Ruling Out the Unknown

Ruling Out the Unknown

Jennifer Kilgrave

CONTENTS

Published by Revitalized Occult and Strange,
an imprint of Bald and Bonkers Network LLC

ISBN: 979-8-3304-2059-9

Understanding the Haunted Home Phenomenon

The History of Haunted Homes

The concept of haunted homes has intrigued human imagination for centuries, with origins deeply rooted in diverse cultural beliefs and folklore. For many societies throughout history, unexplained phenomena within residences were often attributed to the presence of spirits or other supernatural entities. In ancient cultures, it was commonly believed that homes could be inhabited by the spirits of ancestors, prompting rituals and ceremonies aimed at appeasing these ethereal beings. As civilizations progressed, so too did the tales of haunted homes, mirroring societal fears, cultural values, and the mysteries surrounding death. These early stories and beliefs laid the foundation for our ongoing fascination with hauntings, which remains a prominent aspect of contemporary culture.

During the 19th century, the Victorian era witnessed a significant surge in interest regarding hauntings, coinciding with notable advancements in science and a burgeoning curiosity about the afterlife. This period saw the rise of Spiritualism, a movement that popularized the notion that the deceased could communicate with the living. Haunted homes became central to these beliefs, with many individuals reporting ghostly encounters within their residences. This era also marked the beginning of more systematic investigations into hauntings, as people sought to document and understand these phenomena through a blend of scientific inquiry and supernatural exploration.

Despite the rich and varied history of haunted homes, it is essential to approach such claims with a discerning and skeptical perspective. Often, experiences attributed to hauntings can be explained by natural causes, including structural issues, environmental factors, or psychological influences. For example, drafts, creaking floorboards, and faulty wiring can produce noises that may be mistakenly interpreted as ghostly activity. Additionally, the power of suggestion plays a significant role in shaping how individuals perceive their surroundings, leading to heightened awareness of ordinary sounds or sensations when one believes their home is haunted.

To distinguish between natural and supernatural phenomena, individuals can employ a range of investigative techniques when confronted with unexplained noises or disturbances in their homes. One effective approach is meticulous documentation, including recording the time, date, and specific details of each incident. Utilizing technology such as audio recorders or motion sensors can also assist in gathering evidence. By analyzing the collected data, individuals can identify patterns and potential explanations for their experiences, thereby ruling out supernatural causes.

Engaging in a personal investigation of one's home can be both illuminating and empowering. Individuals may benefit from employing tools such as thermometers, electromagnetic field (EMF) meters, and infrared cameras to assess environmental conditions. Cultivating a critical mindset and seeking peer support can further enhance the investigative process. By combining empirical investigation techniques with an understanding of psychological factors that influence perception, individuals can navigate the complex landscape of hauntings and arrive at conclusions based on reality rather than fear or superstition.

Common Myths and Misconceptions

Myths and misconceptions about haunted homes often lead to unnecessary fear and misinterpretation of everyday occurrences. One prevalent myth is that all unexplained noises and sensations are indicative of a haunting. In reality, many sounds attributed to supernatural causes can be explained by natural phenomena such as settling floors, plumbing issues, or structural integrity of the house. Understanding the science behind these noises is crucial for distinguishing between mere coincidence and genuine paranormal activity.

Another common misconception is the belief that a house's history guarantees the presence of spirits. While many people assume that a home with a tragic past is more likely to be haunted, the relationship between a property's history and reported hauntings is not always straightforward. Many homes with dark histories are not haunted, while other residences with no notable past may still have residents who report paranormal experiences. It is essential to evaluate each situation individually, relying on critical thinking and objective analysis rather than solely on anecdotal evidence.

The assumption that feelings of unease or fear in one's home are necessarily due to a haunting often overlooks the psychological factors that can influence perception. Stress, anxiety, and even suggestion can lead individuals to misinterpret ordinary sensations or occurrences as supernatural. By recognizing the role of psychological factors, individuals can better assess their experiences and avoid drawing conclusions based on fear or suggestion.

Additionally, a widespread belief is that spiritual entities thrive on negative energy or fear, which can exacerbate residents' anxieties and contribute to a heightened sense of unease. This myth perpetuates a cycle of fear, further increasing personal anxieties. Understanding that such feelings may stem from psychological or environmental factors rather than supernatural forces can empower individuals to take control of their living spaces and approach their concerns with a rational mindset.

Finally, many people assume that investigating potential hauntings requires expensive tools or specialized training. In truth, a straightforward approach can be highly effective. Basic tools such as notebooks, audio recorders, and even smartphone apps can aid in documenting experiences and identifying patterns over time. By adopting a methodical approach, both skeptics and believers can gather evidence that either supports or refutes the idea of a haunting, leading to a more informed understanding of their environment.

The Appeal of the Supernatural

The allure of the supernatural has captivated human imagination for centuries, often serving as a source of comfort, intrigue, or fear. For those who suspect their homes may be haunted, unexplained phenomena can evoke a complex mix of emotions, including curiosity, anxiety, and excitement. The appeal of the supernatural often lies in its ambiguity, prompting many to jump to conclusions without considering more rational explanations for their experiences. As skeptics, it is crucial to explore the psychological and environmental factors contributing to these perceptions, enabling a clearer understanding of what may truly be occurring within one's home.

One key aspect of the supernatural's appeal is the human tendency to seek patterns and narratives in chaotic or unfamiliar situations. When confronted with strange noises or unsettling occurrences, individuals often search for meaning in these experiences. This psychological phenomenon, known as pareidolia, causes people to perceive familiar shapes or sounds in random stimuli, such as hearing whispers or seeing figures in shadows. Recognizing this inclination can help skeptics better evaluate their experiences and consider alternative explanations that do not involve supernatural elements.

Environmental factors also play a significant role in shaping perceptions of hauntings. Homes naturally produce creaks and groans due to settling, temperature fluctuations, and the movement of materials. These sounds can easily be mistaken for ghostly presences, especially during dark or emotionally charged moments. By understanding the physical properties of their living spaces, individuals can demystify these occurrences and rule out the possibility of hauntings. Investigating the structure of a home, including plumbing, heating, and electrical systems, can reveal many of the sources behind unexplained noises.

Psychological influences, particularly the power of suggestion, cannot be overlooked. If an individual believes their home is haunted, they may be more attuned to and likely to interpret benign occurrences as evidence of the supernatural. This heightened awareness can create a feedback loop, amplifying the perceived evidence of a haunting. By approaching the situation with a skeptical mindset, individuals can mitigate these biases and foster a more objective analysis of their experiences.

Conducting a personal investigation into potential hauntings can offer valuable insights and clarity. Utilizing tools such as audio recorders, thermal imaging cameras, and EMF meters can help differentiate between natural and supernatural explanations. Keeping a detailed log of incidents, including time, date, and environmental conditions, can also aid in identifying patterns that may point to more mundane sources of disturbances. By equipping themselves with knowledge and practical techniques, those who suspect their homes are haunted can navigate the complexities of the supernatural with a rational and informed perspective, ultimately achieving a more accurate understanding of their environment.

2

Ruling Out Your House is Haunted

Identifying Common Causes of Disturbances

Identifying the root causes of disturbances within a home is crucial for anyone who questions the possibility of supernatural phenomena. Often, what initially appears to be paranormal activity can be attributed to more mundane, natural causes. Common disturbances, such as creaking floors, rattling windows, or unexplained noises, can frequently be linked to structural issues or environmental factors. For example, fluctuations in temperature can cause materials like wood to expand or contract, leading to sounds that might be misinterpreted as ghostly activity. Gaining an understanding of these physical properties can significantly aid in distinguishing between the ordinary and the mysterious.

Pests are another common source of disturbances. Rodents, insects, or even birds can create noises that resonate through walls and ceilings, potentially leading homeowners to believe they are experiencing hauntings. Conducting a thorough inspection of the property is essential to identify signs of infestation, such as droppings or nests. By addressing these natural explanations first, one can more accurately focus on other potential causes, ensuring that conclusions about supernatural interference are not drawn prematurely.

Moreover, human psychology plays a pivotal role in how disturbances are perceived. The mind can be particularly susceptible to misinterpretation in environments associated with fear or anxiety. Many individuals report hearing noises or sensing a presence when they are alone or in dimly lit spaces. This phenomenon can be linked to heightened sensory awareness during stressful situations, which often leads to the misinterpretation of ordinary sounds. By understanding these psychological factors, individuals can more accurately assess their experiences and avoid attributing them to the supernatural without substantial evidence.

Electrical issues also frequently contribute to unusual occurrences in a home. Faulty wiring, electrical surges, or malfunctioning appliances can produce buzzing sounds, flickering lights, or even sudden temperature changes. Such factors can easily be mistaken for supernatural phenomena, especially if they coincide with other disturbances. It is advisable to consult a qualified electrician to address any electrical problems before considering the possibility of a haunting.

Finally, environmental factors such as wind, rain, or seismic activity can lead to disturbances that mimic paranormal events. For instance, wind can cause trees to scrape against a house, producing sounds that reverberate through the walls. Similarly, minor tremors or shifts in the earth can generate vibrations that feel unsettling. Conducting a comprehensive investigation of environmental conditions can often reveal these natural causes, leading to a clearer understanding of one's experiences. In summary, by recognizing and addressing these common disturbances, individuals can approach the question of hauntings with a more informed and critical perspective.

The Role of Environmental Factors

Environmental factors play a significant role in shaping our perceptions and experiences, particularly when it comes to phenomena often labeled as supernatural. In the context of haunted homes, understanding these factors can help differentiate between genuine paranormal activity and natural occurrences. From the physical layout of a home to its surrounding environment, numerous elements can contribute to sensations or experiences that might be misconstrued as otherworldly.

One key environmental factor is the presence of mold and other allergens. Research has shown that exposure to certain types of mold can lead to neurological symptoms, including hallucinations and feelings of anxiety. This can create an environment where residents feel uneasy or perceive unusual sounds. Therefore, it is essential for individuals who suspect their homes are haunted to consider whether environmental health issues could be influencing their experiences. Regular inspections and proper ventilation are crucial in mitigating these risks and determining whether discomfort is linked to more mundane sources.

Sound is another significant factor. Homes often have unique acoustics that can amplify or distort noises, leading to misinterpretations. For example, settling noises, creaking floors, or drafts can all produce sounds that might be mistaken for footsteps or whispers. Additionally, environmental conditions such as wind and temperature can impact how sound travels through a home. Conducting a thorough investigation of sound patterns within a residence can help rule out these natural explanations, providing a clearer understanding of the noises one hears.

Lighting conditions also play a role in shaping perceptions of hauntings. Low light levels can create shadows and visual distortions that may be interpreted as figures or movements. Flickering lights or electrical issues can also trigger feelings of unease, leading occupants to believe they are experiencing paranormal events. Ensuring that a home is well-lit and free from electrical malfunctions can reduce the likelihood of these misinterpretations. Keeping a detailed log of visual anomalies along with environmental conditions can assist in determining if what is witnessed has a rational explanation.

Temperature fluctuations are another environmental factor that can contribute to the sensation of being haunted. Sudden drops in temperature are often associated with ghostly encounters, yet they can also be attributed to drafts, poor insulation, or malfunctioning heating systems. Monitoring temperature changes and eliminating potential sources of cold spots can address these sensations logically. Tools such as thermometers and infrared cameras can be valuable in objectively assessing thermal anomalies within a home.

In summary, understanding the role of environmental factors is essential for anyone investigating potential hauntings. By systematically examining aspects such as allergens, sound acoustics, lighting conditions, and temperature variations, individuals can differentiate between natural phenomena and potential supernatural experiences. This critical approach not only demystifies the concept of hauntings but also empowers residents to create a safer and more comfortable living environment.

Assessing Historical Context

Assessing the historical context of a property is a fundamental step for anyone investigating claims of paranormal activity. Understanding a home's past can provide valuable insights into the potential origins of reported phenomena. Many individuals who believe their homes are haunted may not realize that historical occurrences—such as past inhabitants, significant events, or architectural changes—can greatly influence their perceptions of normal sounds and occurrences. Before jumping to conclusions about supernatural activity, it is essential to thoroughly explore the history of the property and its previous occupants.

Begin by researching the home's construction date, previous owners, and any notable events that may have occurred there. Local archives, libraries, and historical societies often house records that can illuminate the past. These may include newspaper articles, property records, and oral histories from long-time residents. Understanding the timeline of your home can help differentiate between natural explanations for unexplained noises and genuine supernatural claims. For example, if a house has a history of tragic events, residents might be more inclined to associate everyday sounds with hauntings, leading to heightened anxiety and sensitivity to their environment.

In addition to the property's history, it is important to consider the cultural and social context in which the home exists. Different communities have varying beliefs about the supernatural, which can shape how residents interpret their experiences. For instance, a family living in an area with a strong tradition of folklore might be more inclined to view unexplained noises as paranormal rather than attributing them to natural causes like settling or pests. Understanding these cultural influences can help skeptics approach their investigations more objectively and recognize how societal beliefs can shape perceptions of hauntings.

Another critical aspect of assessing historical context is examining the psychological factors at play. The mind can be easily influenced, particularly in environments perceived as eerie or unsettling. Stress, grief, or even media portrayals of hauntings can amplify fears and lead to misinterpretations of ordinary phenomena. By considering the psychological state of current residents and their beliefs about the supernatural, investigators can better understand how these elements might contribute to their experiences in the home.

Finally, conducting a personal investigation with a focus on historical context can provide valuable insights. Equip yourself with tools to document findings, such as notebooks, cameras, and audio recorders, to capture any incidents that occur. Maintain a detailed record of the time, place, and circumstances surrounding unexplained occurrences. This meticulous documentation not only aids in ruling out natural causes but also offers a clearer picture of how the home's history interacts with present experiences. By systematically assessing the historical context, individuals can approach their investigation with a balanced perspective, leading to a more informed conclusion about whether their home is genuinely haunted or a product of its past and human perception.

3

Techniques for Investigating Unexplaine

Soundproofing and Noise Reduction

Soundproofing and noise reduction are essential in addressing concerns about potential hauntings within a home. Often, unexplained noises that some might interpret as supernatural can usually be attributed to a variety of natural and environmental factors. Gaining a thorough understanding of how sound travels through a space and implementing effective soundproofing techniques can help demystify these disturbances and offer a clearer perspective on their true sources.

To begin, identifying the sources of noise is a crucial first step in soundproofing a home. Common sources include creaky floorboards, settling foundations, plumbing systems, and even external noises from traffic or wildlife. A systematic investigation of these areas allows homeowners to distinguish between typical household sounds and those that might initially seem unusual. Recording these noises, along with noting their times and locations, can provide valuable insights into their origins, which is crucial for anyone attempting to rule out supernatural explanations.

Incorporating soundproofing materials can significantly mitigate unwanted noise. For example, weather stripping can be added to doors and windows to block external sounds, while acoustic panels installed on walls can absorb noise within a room. Additionally, rugs or carpets can help dampen sounds from footsteps or objects being moved. These modifications not only enhance comfort but also contribute to a quieter environment, making it easier to identify any genuinely unexplained phenomena.

Psychological factors also play a significant role in how individuals perceive noises in their homes. The mind is particularly susceptible to misinterpretation, especially in environments where one feels vulnerable or anxious. Heightened emotions can amplify the perception of sound, leading to ordinary creaks or settling noises being perceived as something more ominous. Maintaining a calm and rational mindset, combined with a well-soundproofed space, can help alleviate anxiety and provide clarity during investigations.

Conducting a personal investigation into unexplained noises can be a fulfilling endeavor, provided the right tools and techniques are utilized. Sound recording devices are invaluable for capturing noises that might otherwise go unnoticed. By combining these recordings with soundproofing measures, investigators can create a more controlled environment for their research. Systematically eliminating potential sound sources and focusing on what remains allows homeowners to better understand their living space, leading to a more informed conclusion about whether their home is truly haunted or merely affected by natural sound phenomena.

Recording and Analyzing Sounds

Recording and analyzing sounds is a vital step for anyone investigating potential paranormal activity in their home. The first task is to capture clear audio recordings of the unexplained noises. This can be achieved using various recording devices, ranging from high-quality digital recorders to smartphone applications. It is important to ensure that the recording equipment is properly set up to capture the best possible sound quality. For optimal results, record during a quiet period when background noise is minimized to avoid contaminating the audio.

Once the sounds are recorded, critical analysis is the next step. This involves listening to the recordings multiple times and taking detailed notes on the characteristics of the sounds. Pay attention to factors such as frequency, duration, intensity, and any discernible patterns. For instance, a single creak followed by silence may differ significantly from a series of rapid taps. Identifying these characteristics can help distinguish between natural occurrences, such as a house settling, and sounds that might be more challenging to explain.

Environmental factors should also be considered when analyzing recorded sounds. Temperature and humidity changes can cause materials in a house to expand or contract, producing noises that could be mistaken for something supernatural. Additionally, external factors like wind, wildlife, or nearby construction can generate sounds that travel into your home and may be misinterpreted as paranormal. Keeping a detailed log of both the recorded sounds and the environmental conditions can assist in determining if there is a logical explanation for the noises.

Psychological factors play a significant role in how individuals perceive and interpret sounds. The mind has a tendency to fill in gaps and create narratives, especially in contexts of fear or anxiety. If someone believes their home is haunted, they may be more inclined to attribute ordinary sounds to supernatural causes. It is crucial to approach sound analysis with an objective mindset, being mindful of one's own biases and preconceptions. This awareness helps prevent misinterpretation and fosters a more rational understanding of the sounds.

A balanced approach to personal investigation involves both skepticism and open-mindedness. Utilizing sound analysis software can enhance the investigation by allowing for the visualization of sound waves and identification of anomalies that might not be immediately obvious to the ear. Engaging with other skeptics or paranormal enthusiasts can provide additional perspectives and insights. Thorough recording and analysis of sounds lead to a greater understanding of what is occurring in your home, helping to rule out unknown factors in a logical and methodical manner.

Engaging Neighbors and Community

Interacting with neighbors and the local community can yield important insights and support when exploring possible hauntings. Often, unexplained noises or events have logical explanations based on environmental factors and the experiences of nearby residents. Engaging with neighbors allows for the collection of firsthand accounts of similar events, aiding in the differentiation between actual supernatural occurrences and explainable natural phenomena. This shared knowledge contributes to a more comprehensive understanding of the neighborhood's history and collective experiences, leading to a more informed approach to personal inquiries.

In conversations about unexplained events, it's crucial to remain sensitive and open-minded. Neighbors may have varying beliefs or skepticism regarding the supernatural. Cultivating respectful communication fosters an atmosphere where experiences and observations can be freely shared, improving the understanding of potential environmental influences like construction, wildlife, or local legends on these occurrences. Encouraging the sharing of personal stories strengthens community bonds and assists in dispelling misconceptions about hauntings.

Furthermore, organizing community gatherings offers a venue for discussing unexplained events. Workshops or discussion groups that delve into local history, architecture, and environmental elements can provide a backdrop for residents' perceptions of hauntings. Including local historians or specialists can enhance these events, offering insights into the structural features of homes and neighborhoods that may shape residents' experiences. This collective effort can clarify misunderstandings about hauntings and enable individuals to approach their concerns with a deeper comprehension of their environment.

Psychological factors significantly influence how individuals perceive their environments. Engaging with neighbors can reveal shared psychological triggers that may impact perceptions of hauntings. For instance, stress, fatigue, or recent life changes can heighten sensitivity to sounds and sensations that might otherwise go unnoticed. Open discussions within the community can provide a more nuanced perspective on these experiences. Understanding that one is not alone in their feelings can help dispel fears and anxiety, revealing that experiences may stem from common psychological patterns rather than supernatural forces.

Ultimately, fostering a sense of community is instrumental in demystifying the experience of potential hauntings. Collaborating with neighbors enables individuals to share tools and techniques for personal investigations, creating a network of support that promotes critical thinking over fear. This collective effort not only aids in ruling out supernatural explanations but also strengthens community bonds. As residents work together to uncover the truth behind their experiences, they may find camaraderie in their shared journey, transforming what initially seemed like a haunting into an opportunity for connection and mutual understanding.

4

Differences in Natural and Supernatural Phenomenon

Understanding Natural Explanations

Understanding natural explanations for phenomena that are often attributed to hauntings is crucial for anyone seeking to rule out the possibility of a supernatural presence in their home. Many people experiencing unexplained noises or sensations may jump to conclusions based on fear or preconceived notions about the paranormal. However, a deeper investigation into the natural causes of these experiences can provide clarity and peace of mind. By examining common environmental factors, psychological influences, and scientific principles, one can gain a more rational perspective on what might be occurring in their living space.

One of the primary natural explanations for strange sounds or occurrences in a home is the impact of environmental factors. Old houses, in particular, can produce creaks and groans due to settling, temperature changes, and the expansion and contraction of materials. Pipes may rattle, floors may shift, and even the wind can create eerie sounds that resemble whispers or footsteps. Understanding how structural elements interact with the environment can help demystify these noises and prevent unwarranted fear. Keeping a record of specific occurrences and correlating them with weather patterns or household activities can offer further insight into their origins.

Another significant aspect to consider is the psychological factors that contribute to perceptions of hauntings. Human brains are wired to recognize patterns and seek explanations for the unknown. This tendency can lead individuals to interpret ambiguous stimuli as supernatural, especially in high-stress situations or during emotional distress. The phenomenon known as pareidolia, where people see faces or figures in random patterns, can also play a role in how we perceive our surroundings. By understanding these cognitive biases, individuals can better assess their experiences without jumping to supernatural conclusions.

To investigate unexplained noises or sensations effectively, one can employ various techniques and tools designed to identify natural causes. Recording devices can capture sounds for later analysis, while thermal imaging cameras can help detect temperature fluctuations that may indicate drafts or malfunctioning heating systems. Keeping a detailed log of experiences, including time, location, and context, can reveal patterns that assist in identifying the source of disturbances. Engaging in a methodical approach to investigation can demystify the unknown and lead to more rational explanations.

In conclusion, by prioritizing an understanding of natural explanations over supernatural assumptions, individuals can approach their experiences with a more skeptical and informed mindset. Researching common environmental factors, recognizing the influence of psychological processes, and utilizing effective investigation techniques will empower homeowners to differentiate between natural and supernatural phenomena. This analytical approach not only provides clarity but can also foster a greater sense of control and comfort within one's living environment.

The Science of Perception

Perception is a complex process that involves not only the reception of sensory information but also the interpretation of that information based on our beliefs, experiences, and expectations. This is particularly relevant in the context of haunted homes, where unexplained noises and eerie sensations can easily be misinterpreted. Understanding the science of perception can help individuals differentiate between genuine supernatural occurrences and natural explanations. By recognizing the cognitive biases that shape our perceptions, we can better navigate the realm of the unexplained and rule out the possibility of a haunting.

One significant aspect of perception is the role of context. Our brains are wired to interpret stimuli based on the surrounding environment. In a dimly lit room, for instance, a creaking floorboard may evoke feelings of dread, leading to assumptions of a ghostly presence. Conversely, in a brightly lit and familiar space, the same sound might be dismissed as an ordinary occurrence. This highlights the importance of context when investigating perceived hauntings; familiarizing oneself with the environment and its history can provide critical insights that mitigate fear-driven interpretations.

Another crucial factor is the concept of cognitive biases, such as confirmation bias, which can lead individuals to favor information that aligns with their pre-existing beliefs about the supernatural. When investigating unexplained noises, skeptics must strive to remain objective, seeking evidence that both supports and contradicts their initial beliefs. By maintaining a balanced perspective, individuals can better assess whether the sounds they hear are truly supernatural or simply products of their imagination and environmental factors.

Psychological factors also play a significant role in shaping our perceptions of hauntings. Stress, anxiety, and even sleep deprivation can heighten sensitivity to environmental stimuli, making mundane noises seem more pronounced or sinister. Additionally, the power of suggestion can not be underestimated; if someone enters a home with the belief that it is haunted, they are more likely to perceive strange occurrences as paranormal. Acknowledging these psychological influences can help individuals take a step back and evaluate their experiences more critically.

When conducting a personal investigation into perceived hauntings, several tools and techniques can aid in ruling out the unknown. Utilizing digital sound recorders, infrared cameras, and even simple notepads can assist in documenting occurrences and analyzing patterns over time. Moreover, engaging in discussions with family members or friends can provide alternative perspectives that may reveal natural explanations for the noises. By systematically collecting data and remaining open to various interpretations, individuals can cultivate a more informed understanding of their experiences, ultimately leading to a more rational conclusion about whether their home is truly haunted.

Case Studies of Misidentified Hauntings

Case studies of misidentified hauntings provide valuable insights into how seemingly paranormal experiences can often be explained through natural or psychological phenomena. One notable example occurred in a well-documented case in a historic home in Massachusetts. Residents reported disembodied voices and strange footsteps in the attic. Initial investigations suggested possible haunting activity. However, a closer examination revealed that the sounds were emanating from an old heating system, which was malfunctioning and producing creaking noises that mimicked footfalls. This case underscores the importance of thorough investigations, as what may initially appear to be paranormal can often be attributed to mundane causes.

Another instance involved a family in a suburban neighborhood who believed their home was haunted due to frequent unexplained cold spots and flickering lights. Upon conducting a detailed investigation, it was discovered that the house had inadequate insulation and outdated electrical wiring. The cold spots were the result of drafts from poorly sealed windows, while the flickering lights were traced to loose connections in the electrical fixtures. This case highlights how environmental factors can influence perceptions of a haunting, illustrating the need for homeowners to consider physical conditions before jumping to supernatural conclusions.

Psychological factors play a significant role in the interpretation of unexplained phenomena. In a case from a small town in Oregon, a couple reported seeing shadowy figures and feeling an ominous presence in their home. However, interviews with the residents revealed that they had recently experienced a traumatic event, which heightened their sensitivity to their surroundings. A psychological evaluation indicated that their heightened state of anxiety contributed to their perception of the environment as threatening. This example emphasizes how mental and emotional states can skew one's interpretation of experiences, leading to misidentification of hauntings.

Another compelling case involved a historical inn in Georgia, where guests frequently reported ghostly encounters. Upon investigation, it was revealed that the inn's architecture created unique acoustic phenomena, amplifying sounds from outside. Additionally, the staff conducted a survey and found that many guests were influenced by the inn's ghostly marketing, which shaped their expectations and experiences. The research suggested that the anticipation of experiencing the supernatural led guests to misinterpret ordinary sounds and movements as paranormal activity. This demonstrates the significant impact of suggestion and expectation in the perception of hauntings.

Finally, a case study from a family living near a wooded area illustrates how wildlife can contribute to perceptions of a haunted environment. The family frequently heard rustling noises at night and believed they were encountering spirits. However, an investigation revealed that the sounds were caused by raccoons and other nocturnal animals foraging near their home. This case serves as a reminder that the natural world can often be mistaken for the supernatural. By understanding the potential sources of unexplained noises and experiences, individuals can better distinguish between natural phenomena and claims of hauntings, ultimately fostering a more rational approach to investigating the unknown.

5

Psychological Factors in Perceptions of Hauntings

The Role of Suggestibility

The concept of suggestibility plays a crucial role in shaping our perceptions of unexplained phenomena, particularly in the context of haunted homes. Suggestibility refers to the degree to which individuals are influenced by external cues or suggestions, often leading them to interpret experiences in ways that align with those suggestions. In environments where reports of paranormal activity abound, such as homes believed to be haunted, people may become more susceptible to suggestion, affecting their interpretations of sounds, sights, and sensations. Understanding this psychological phenomenon is essential for anyone investigating or experiencing potential hauntings.

When individuals enter a space with preconceived notions of it being haunted, their perceptions can be significantly altered. The mind often seeks to confirm existing beliefs, leading to a cycle of suggestion that reinforces the idea of supernatural occurrences. For instance, if a homeowner has read stories about ghosts in their neighborhood, they may begin to interpret ordinary creaks and groans of their house as evidence of paranormal activity. This can create a feedback loop where heightened awareness of potential haunting leads to increased suggestibility, further distorting perceptions of reality.

Moreover, the setting itself can amplify suggestibility. Dim lighting, unfamiliar surroundings, and even the time of day can influence how people interpret sensory input. For example, being alone in a dark, quiet room may heighten feelings of anxiety and fear, causing an individual to misinterpret benign noises as ghostly presences. The powerful impact of suggestion can lead to misperceptions, where natural explanations for sounds—such as settling wood or plumbing—are overshadowed by the expectation of encountering something supernatural.

To effectively rule out the possibility of a haunting, skeptics should employ strategies that mitigate the effects of suggestibility. One effective approach is to conduct an investigation with a clear, rational mindset and to gather evidence before jumping to conclusions. Utilizing tools such as audio recorders or motion detectors can help document occurrences objectively. By focusing on empirical data rather than subjective experiences, individuals can create a more balanced understanding of their environment, thereby reducing the influence of suggestion on their interpretations.

Finally, it is essential to recognize the psychological factors that contribute to perceptions of hauntings. Awareness of suggestibility can empower individuals to approach their experiences with a critical lens, leading to more grounded conclusions about their homes. Engaging in open discussions with skeptics and seeking diverse perspectives can also help counteract the effects of suggestibility. By fostering a rational environment and focusing on evidence-based investigations, homeowners can distinguish between natural phenomena and the supernatural, ultimately leading to a clearer understanding of their living spaces.

Cognitive Biases and Belief Systems

Cognitive biases significantly influence how individuals interpret experiences, particularly when it comes to phenomena that defy explanation, such as potential hauntings. These biases can skew perception, leading individuals to draw conclusions based on flawed reasoning rather than objective analysis. For instance, confirmation bias may lead someone to focus solely on evidence that supports their belief in the supernatural while dismissing contradictory information. This can create a feedback loop that reinforces the belief in hauntings, even in the face of logical explanations. Understanding these biases is crucial for anyone who suspects their home is haunted and seeks to investigate the matter with a critical mindset.

Belief systems also play a vital role in shaping perceptions of unexplained noises and events in the home. Cultural and personal backgrounds can predispose individuals to interpret experiences in a supernatural context. For example, someone raised in a culture rich with ghost stories may be more inclined to view strange sounds as evidence of a haunting, whereas someone with a scientific background may seek out rational explanations first. Recognizing one's own belief system can aid in maintaining a balanced approach when investigating potential hauntings, allowing for a more thorough examination of all possible explanations.

When investigating unexplained noises, it is essential to distinguish between natural and supernatural phenomena. Many sounds attributed to hauntings can be explained by common household occurrences—creaky floorboards, plumbing issues, or even the settling of a house. By employing critical thinking and a systematic approach to investigation, individuals can rule out these natural explanations before considering more extraordinary theories. Utilizing tools such as sound recorders or motion detectors can help in documenting occurrences and analyzing them objectively, minimizing the influence of cognitive biases.

Psychological factors also contribute significantly to perceptions of hauntings. Stress, anxiety, and fatigue can heighten sensitivity to environmental stimuli, making normal sounds more pronounced and potentially eerie. In addition, the power of suggestion can lead individuals to perceive experiences differently based on prior beliefs or expectations. For example, if someone enters a room believing it is haunted, they may interpret a simple draft as a ghostly presence. By fostering awareness of these psychological influences, skeptics can better navigate their experiences and maintain a rational perspective during their investigations.

Conducting a personal investigation requires a blend of skepticism and open-mindedness. Equipped with the knowledge of cognitive biases and belief systems, individuals can approach their inquiries with a critical eye. It is essential to document experiences meticulously, noting details such as time, location, and any potential external factors that could influence perceptions. By applying structured methods to collect and analyze data, individuals can create a clearer picture of their experiences and either rule out or substantiate their concerns about potential hauntings. This rational approach not only demystifies the unknown but also empowers individuals to confront their fears with confidence.

The Impact of Stress and Trauma

The understanding of stress and trauma plays a crucial role in the investigation of purported hauntings. Many individuals who believe their homes are haunted often report feelings of anxiety, fear, and unease. These emotional states can significantly distort perception, leading to misinterpretations of ordinary sounds and sensations as paranormal events. The human brain is wired to react to stress, often triggering a fight-or-flight response that can heighten sensitivity to environmental stimuli. This heightened awareness may cause residents to perceive creaking floors, settling noises, or even their own thoughts as manifestations of supernatural activity.

Traumatic experiences can further complicate one's perception of their living environment. Individuals who have faced significant stress or trauma may be more susceptible to feeling a presence or sensing an unusual atmosphere in their homes. Past experiences can create a psychological lens through which one views their surroundings, often leading to the belief that their home is haunted. This is particularly true in cases where a person has experienced loss, grief, or a major life change, which can amplify feelings of vulnerability and fear in familiar spaces.

Moreover, the psychological ramifications of stress and trauma can lead to the phenomenon known as pareidolia, where the mind perceives familiar patterns or figures in random stimuli. This can manifest in seeing shadows out of the corner of one's eye, hearing whispers when no one is present, or feeling as though someone is watching. Supernatural skeptics must consider these psychological factors when investigating unexplained noises or sensations. By understanding the science behind how stress and trauma affect perception, one can more accurately discern between natural and supernatural phenomena.

When conducting a personal investigation into the possibility of a haunting, it is essential to approach the situation with a critical mindset. Utilizing tools such as audio recorders, night vision cameras, and electromagnetic field detectors can help document occurrences that may seem paranormal. However, it is equally important to maintain an awareness of one's mental state. Keeping a log of emotional responses alongside documented events can provide insight into whether stress and trauma are influencing perceptions of the home. This dual approach can help distinguish between genuine phenomena and those influenced by psychological factors.

Ultimately, recognizing the impact of stress and trauma is vital for anyone seeking to rule out the possibility of a haunting in their home. By applying a rational framework to experiences that may initially appear supernatural, individuals can find peace of mind and a clearer understanding of their environment. This understanding empowers skeptics and believers alike to approach the mysteries of their homes with a balanced perspective, enabling them to explore the unknown while remaining grounded in reality.

6

Conducting Personal Investigations: Tools and Tips

Essential Tools for Home Investigations

When embarking on a home investigation to determine whether unexplained occurrences are truly supernatural, having the right tools at your disposal is crucial. While the perception of hauntings can often stem from psychological factors, it is essential to approach the investigation with a clear mind and a systematic methodology. Common tools that skeptics can utilize include audio recorders, thermometers, and motion detectors. These instruments can help document environmental conditions and capture potential evidence of disturbances, facilitating a thorough analysis of the situation without jumping to conclusions.

Audio recorders are invaluable for capturing unexplained noises that may occur in your home. These devices can pick up sounds that might go unnoticed during the day-to-day hustle and bustle. To maximize their effectiveness, it is advisable to leave recorders running during quiet hours, ideally at night when disturbances are more likely to occur. By reviewing the recordings, you can determine whether the sounds have rational explanations, such as the settling of the house, creaking pipes, or pets moving about. The key is to listen critically and remain open to logical explanations.

Thermometers, particularly infrared models, can help detect sudden temperature fluctuations that some associate with paranormal activity. Cold spots, often reported in haunted locations, may indicate drafts, poor insulation, or even electrical issues. When using a thermometer, it is essential to take consistent measurements in various areas of the home to establish a baseline. Any anomalies in temperature should be cross-referenced with potential sources of drafts or other environmental factors. This process can help distinguish between the effects of natural phenomena and perceived supernatural occurrences.

Motion detectors can further assist in your investigation by identifying movements within specific areas of the home. These devices can be set to monitor rooms where unexplained phenomena are reported. When analyzing the data, consider the possibility of pets, family members, or environmental factors triggering the sensors. It is also important to ensure that the detectors are functioning properly and not overly sensitive, which can lead to false positives. A careful review of the recorded activities will help clarify whether any unusual movements warrant further investigation.

Conducting a personal investigation is not just about the tools used; it also involves maintaining a skeptical mindset throughout the process. Psychological factors can heavily influence perceptions of hauntings, leading individuals to attribute ordinary occurrences to supernatural causes. Keeping a detailed log of experiences, including dates, times, and environmental conditions, allows for a more objective analysis. By employing these essential tools and techniques, skeptics can effectively rule out the possibility of a haunting, grounding their inquiry in rationality and evidence rather than speculation.

Methodologies for Systematic Investigation

Methodologies for systematic investigation are essential for anyone seeking to determine whether unexplained phenomena in their home can be attributed to natural causes rather than supernatural ones. A structured approach not only helps in gathering reliable evidence but also in analyzing that evidence critically. The first step involves identifying specific occurrences that raise concern, such as strange noises, cold spots, or feelings of unease. Documenting these experiences meticulously will provide a foundation for understanding their frequency, duration, and potential triggers. This initial data collection is crucial for differentiating between genuine anomalies and those that may be influenced by psychological factors or environmental conditions.

Once data has been collected, the next methodology involves conducting a thorough environmental examination. This includes assessing the physical characteristics of the home that could explain unusual occurrences. For example, examining the structure for drafts, plumbing issues, or electrical anomalies can often reveal the source of sounds or temperature fluctuations that may initially appear paranormal. Additionally, using tools such as thermometers, sound recorders, and motion detectors can help document environmental changes during specific incidents. Understanding these variables allows investigators to rule out natural explanations before considering supernatural ones.

Another critical aspect of systematic investigation is the psychological dimension. Human perception plays a significant role in how we interpret experiences within our homes. Factors such as stress, fatigue, and cultural beliefs can influence our reactions to unexplained occurrences. Engaging in discussions with family members or friends about their experiences can help identify common themes or misinterpretations. It is essential to approach these conversations with an open mind while remaining skeptical of anecdotal evidence that lacks corroboration. Recognizing the psychological components of perception will strengthen the overall investigation and reduce the likelihood of jumping to supernatural conclusions.

Conducting a personal investigation requires not only a methodical approach but also practical tools and tips to enhance the effectiveness of the inquiry. Setting up a regular schedule for monitoring occurrences can help establish patterns over time. Utilizing smartphone apps designed for paranormal investigations may provide additional insights, such as EMF detectors or sound analysis tools. However, it is crucial to remain critical of the data these tools provide, as they can be influenced by environmental factors. Keeping a detailed log of findings, including dates, times, and conditions during each event, will assist in creating a comprehensive overview of the situation.

Finally, after gathering substantial evidence and analyzing it through various methodologies, it is important to synthesize the findings. This synthesis should focus on distinguishing between natural and supernatural explanations, assessing the weight of the evidence, and drawing informed conclusions. Engaging with skeptical literature and expert opinions can further enhance understanding and provide context for the findings. By maintaining a systematic investigation approach, individuals can arrive at a reasoned conclusion about their home's unexplained phenomena, empowering them to address their concerns logically and effectively.

Documenting Findings Effectively

Documenting findings effectively is a crucial aspect of investigating claims of hauntings, particularly for those who approach the subject with skepticism. Accurate documentation allows investigators to establish a clear record of events, observations, and conclusions drawn during the investigation. This process begins with creating a structured format for recording experiences, which can include date, time, location, and a detailed description of the phenomena encountered. Including environmental conditions, such as temperature and humidity, can provide valuable context for any findings. By maintaining consistency in documentation, investigators can later analyze patterns or correlations that may emerge over time.

When investigating unexplained noises, it is essential to employ a systematic approach to capturing audio evidence. Using quality recording equipment, such as digital voice recorders, can help ensure that sounds are recorded clearly. It is advisable to document the location and conditions under which the recording took place, including any background noise that may interfere with the clarity of the captured sound. Additionally, reviewing the audio in a controlled environment can help distinguish between natural sounds and those that may appear supernatural. By meticulously logging these details, skeptics can critically assess the validity of the recorded evidence.

In addition to audio recordings, visual documentation plays a significant role in investigating claims of hauntings. Photographs and video recordings can provide valuable insights into the environment being examined. It is important to document the settings before, during, and after any notable occurrences. Utilizing time-stamped photographs ensures that any anomalies can be correlated with specific events or environmental changes. When reviewing visual evidence, skeptics should remain vigilant for common optical illusions or reflections that can easily be mistaken for supernatural phenomena. Thorough documentation of these variables aids in the objective analysis of visual claims.

Psychological factors also contribute to the perception of hauntings, and documenting the emotional state of witnesses can provide context for their experiences. Keeping a journal of personal interviews can help capture the nuances of individual perceptions and interpretations of events. It is vital to note any suggestive circumstances, such as prior knowledge of the property's history or exposure to media depicting hauntings, which may influence a person's experiences. By compiling this psychological data alongside environmental and experiential evidence, investigators can develop a more comprehensive understanding of the phenomena being reported.

Finally, conducting a personal investigation requires the right tools and techniques for effective documentation. Utilizing checklists during investigations can ensure that no detail is overlooked. Consider including sections for recording personal observations, environmental measurements, and any equipment readings. The use of technology, such as thermal imaging cameras or electromagnetic field meters, can also enhance the quality of documentation. After the investigation, compiling all findings into a coherent report allows for easier analysis and discussion. This report should include summaries of the documented evidence alongside an objective assessment of the data, encouraging skepticism and critical thinking in the evaluation of potential hauntings.

7

When to Seek Professional Help

Recognizing Serious Issues

Recognizing serious issues within a home that is suspected of being haunted requires a systematic approach to differentiate between natural occurrences and potential supernatural phenomena. Many individuals experience unexplained noises, cold spots, or feelings of being watched, leading them to consider the possibility of a haunting. However, before jumping to conclusions, it is essential to investigate these occurrences critically. This involves understanding the common causes of such phenomena, which can often be attributed to environmental factors, structural issues, or psychological influences.

Unexplained noises, the most frequently reported phenomenon in suspected haunted locations, can often be traced back to natural sources. These may include settling of the house, plumbing issues, or electrical problems. For instance, creaking floorboards may simply be the result of temperature changes affecting the materials in the home. Conducting a thorough inspection of the property can help identify these issues. Listening carefully during different times of the day and noting any patterns in the sounds may provide clarity. Keeping a detailed log of these occurrences can also assist in determining whether the noises correlate with specific events or environmental conditions.

Psychological factors play a significant role in how individuals perceive their surroundings. Stress, anxiety, and even suggestibility can amplify the feeling of unease in a home. When people believe their house is haunted, they may become hyper-aware of their environment, interpreting ordinary sounds and sights as supernatural. It is crucial for individuals to engage in self-reflection and assess their mental state when experiencing these phenomena. Additionally, speaking with family members or friends can provide an outside perspective, helping to identify any irrational fears or exaggerated perceptions.

Conducting a personal investigation into potential hauntings involves utilizing tools and techniques that can aid in discerning between natural and supernatural explanations. Simple tools such as a digital voice recorder, thermometer, and infrared camera can be valuable in documenting experiences. Setting up these devices in areas where unusual occurrences are reported can help capture evidence. Moreover, employing the use of a journal to note observations, including weather conditions and personal feelings at the time of these events, can contribute to a more comprehensive understanding of the situation.

In conclusion, recognizing serious issues in a suspected haunted home requires a blend of critical thinking, systematic investigation, and self-awareness. By ruling out natural explanations for unexplained occurrences, individuals can alleviate fears and misconceptions surrounding their living environment. This process not only demystifies the home but also empowers residents to create a more comfortable and peaceful atmosphere. Through diligence and an open mind, the truth behind their experiences can be uncovered, leading to a deeper understanding of both the physical and psychological aspects of their home.

Evaluating Paranormal Investigators

When evaluating paranormal investigators, it is essential to approach the process with a critical mindset. Many self-proclaimed paranormal experts claim to possess the ability to determine whether a property is haunted. However, not all investigators adhere to rigorous standards or scientific methods. To assess their credibility, consider their qualifications, experience, and the methodologies they employ. Investigators should ideally have a background in fields such as psychology, physics, or environmental science, which can provide them with the necessary tools to analyze potential hauntings from a rational perspective rather than relying solely on anecdotal evidence.

One of the most critical aspects of evaluating a paranormal investigator is their approach to evidence collection. A reliable investigator will utilize various tools, such as electromagnetic field (EMF) meters, digital voice recorders, and infrared cameras, to gather data during an investigation. However, it is important to question how they interpret this evidence. Investigators should be transparent about their findings, offering clear explanations for any anomalies encountered, rather than jumping to supernatural conclusions. A good investigator will also acknowledge the possibility of natural explanations for the phenomena, demonstrating a balanced approach to their work.

A credible paranormal investigator should also exhibit a strong understanding of the psychological factors that can influence perceptions of hauntings. Many individuals experiencing unexplained noises or feelings of unease in their homes may be influenced by their beliefs, fears, or even environmental stressors. Investigators should be able to discuss these psychological aspects openly and consider them when evaluating a case. By recognizing the role of human perception in interpreting supernatural occurrences, they can provide a more comprehensive analysis that goes beyond mere ghost-hunting.

When selecting a paranormal investigator, consider their communication skills and willingness to engage in dialogue with clients. A professional investigator should prioritize understanding the homeowner's experiences, allowing them to express their concerns and feelings fully. This empathetic approach is vital to building trust and ensuring that the investigator can address the homeowner's needs effectively. Investigators who dismiss clients' experiences or fail to listen may not provide the thorough evaluation that is necessary to rule out the possibility of a haunting.

Lastly, it is essential to investigate the reputation of a paranormal investigator within the community. Look for reviews, testimonials, and references from previous clients. A reputable investigator will have a history of conducting thorough investigations and providing clients with comprehensive reports outlining their findings. Additionally, consider whether they are involved in ongoing education within the field, as this demonstrates a commitment to improving their skills and knowledge. By taking the time to evaluate potential investigators carefully, homeowners can make informed decisions that ultimately help them discern the true nature of their experiences.

Alternatives to Traditional Investigations

In the realm of investigating potential hauntings, traditional methods often rely heavily on anecdotal evidence and personal testimonies. However, there are several alternatives that can provide a more structured and analytical approach to understanding unexplained phenomena within one's home. These alternatives focus on scientific inquiry, psychological evaluation, and environmental analysis, allowing skeptics and believers alike to explore their experiences with a critical eye. By employing these methods, individuals can better distinguish between natural occurrences and potential supernatural influences.

One effective alternative is employing technology to monitor environmental changes. Tools such as digital thermometers, sound level meters, and motion sensors can help document fluctuations in temperature, sound, and movement. For instance, unexplained cold spots often attributed to ghostly presences can be measured with precise instruments, allowing for a more objective analysis. By systematically recording these variables, individuals can create a baseline of their home's typical environmental conditions, making it easier to identify anomalies that may have logical explanations, such as drafts or electrical issues.

Another valuable approach involves psychological factors that can influence perceptions of hauntings. Understanding the psychological state of those who experience unexplained phenomena is crucial. Factors such as stress, fatigue, and suggestibility can significantly impact how individuals interpret their surroundings. Engaging in mindfulness practices or cognitive behavioral techniques can help individuals assess their mental state and reduce the likelihood of misinterpreting normal occurrences as supernatural events. This self-reflection can be an essential step in distinguishing between genuine hauntings and the mind's tendency to create narratives based on fear or anxiety.

Conducting personal investigations with a structured methodology can also yield significant insights. Creating a detailed log of occurrences, including time, date, and environmental conditions, allows individuals to identify patterns over time. This systematic approach can help discern whether phenomena are recurring or isolated incidents. Additionally, involving friends or family members in the investigation can provide different perspectives, reducing the likelihood of confirmation bias. Diverse viewpoints can help challenge assumptions and lead to a more comprehensive understanding of the situation.

Finally, engaging with local experts or community resources can enhance the investigation process. Connecting with paranormal research groups or local historians can provide valuable insights into the history of the home and its previous occupants. These resources may offer explanations for certain phenomena that are rooted in historical events or local folklore. Furthermore, they can assist in analyzing evidence collected during personal investigations, offering a broader context and potentially debunking myths associated with haunted locations. By combining these alternative methods, individuals can approach their experiences with a balanced perspective, grounded in both skepticism and curiosity.

8

Moving Forward: Living in Your Home

Coping Strategies for Residents

Dealing with the fear and uncertainty that comes with the suspicion of a haunted home necessitates a practical approach. It's beneficial for residents to develop strategies that enable them to differentiate between ordinary events and those that might be considered supernatural. The initial step involves staying calm and logical in the face of unexplained disturbances. A composed mindset allows for a more objective analysis of events, preventing panic and irrational fears that can distort perception and lead to false interpretations.

An effective method is maintaining a comprehensive record of any unusual incidents. This record should detail the dates, times, and descriptions of these events, along with any relevant factors like weather conditions or local activities. As this log grows, patterns may become apparent, providing insights into natural explanations for these disturbances. For example, the noise of expanding and contracting floorboards could correlate with changes in humidity, or plumbing sounds may be more noticeable during the quiet of the night. Documenting these details helps residents understand their surroundings better and diminishes concerns about hauntings.

In addition to logging occurrences, utilizing a variety of investigative tools can enhance residents' ability to discern natural phenomena from the supernatural. Simple devices such as voice recorders, temperature gauges, and motion sensors can aid in capturing evidence of unexplained sounds or movements. Learning how to use these tools effectively can empower residents to conduct their own investigations, leading to more informed conclusions. Moreover, using technology to record experiences can provide a sense of control over the situation, helping to alleviate feelings of helplessness that often accompany fears of hauntings.

It is equally important for residents to recognize the psychological factors that play a role in their perceptions of hauntings. Stress, anxiety, and fatigue can significantly influence how individuals interpret their surroundings. Engaging in mindfulness practices can help ground residents in the present moment, allowing them to separate their fears from reality. Additionally, discussing their experiences with friends or family can provide emotional support and alternative perspectives that may help to demystify their feelings of unease. Sharing these experiences can foster a sense of community and reduce the isolation that often accompanies fears of the unknown.

Finally, seeking professional help when necessary is a crucial coping strategy. If a resident finds that their fears are overwhelming or negatively impacting their quality of life, consulting with a mental health professional can provide valuable support. Therapy can assist individuals in addressing underlying anxieties and developing healthier coping mechanisms. In some cases, professionals trained in environmental psychology may offer insights into how one's living space can influence feelings of discomfort. By combining self-investigation with professional guidance, residents can develop a comprehensive approach to coping with their fears, ultimately leading to a greater sense of peace and understanding regarding their home environment.

Creating a Peaceful Living Environment

Creating a peaceful living environment is essential for anyone concerned about the possibility of hauntings. To rule out supernatural disturbances, it is crucial to establish a calm and serene atmosphere in your home. This can be achieved by addressing environmental factors that contribute to anxiety, stress, and fear, which can amplify perceptions of unexplained noises and other phenomena. By focusing on creating a soothing space, you not only help alleviate your concerns but also provide a clearer context for investigating any unusual occurrences.

One effective way to foster tranquility in your living environment is to reduce clutter and organize your space. Clutter can create feelings of chaos and unease, making it difficult to distinguish between natural and supernatural phenomena. By decluttering, you not only improve the aesthetics of your home but also enhance your mental clarity. A tidy space allows for easier observation of your surroundings, making it simpler to identify the source of any strange sounds or occurrences without the distraction of disorganization.

Incorporating elements of nature into your living space can also promote peace and a sense of grounding. Plants, natural light, and serene colors contribute to a calming atmosphere. The presence of greenery has been shown to reduce stress and improve overall well-being. Additionally, natural light helps regulate mood and energy levels, creating a more inviting environment. When your home feels more like a sanctuary, you are better equipped to approach any potential hauntings from a rational standpoint, focusing on investigation rather than fear.

Soundproofing your home can mitigate the impact of external noises that may be mistaken for ghostly disturbances. Unexplained sounds often lead to heightened anxiety and suspicion about the supernatural. By identifying and addressing sources of noise, such as drafts, creaky floors, or even plumbing issues, you can significantly reduce the likelihood of misinterpreting these sounds. Techniques such as using rugs to dampen sound or sealing gaps around windows and doors can create a quieter environment, allowing for a more accurate assessment of any unexplained phenomena.

Lastly, fostering a positive mental attitude is vital for creating a peaceful living environment. Psychological factors play a significant role in perceptions of hauntings. Engaging in mindfulness practices, such as meditation or yoga, can help calm the mind and reduce anxiety. A relaxed state allows you to approach any unusual occurrences with a critical and open mindset. When you maintain a peaceful demeanor, it becomes easier to conduct a personal investigation into any unexplained noises, focusing on logical explanations rather than jumping to supernatural conclusions. By cultivating tranquility in your home, you empower yourself to discern the unknown with clarity and confidence.

Embracing Skepticism in Daily Life

Embracing skepticism in daily life is an essential practice, particularly for those who find themselves grappling with the unnerving possibility of a haunted home. Skepticism encourages a critical examination of experiences that might otherwise lead to unwarranted conclusions. By applying a skeptical lens, individuals can differentiate between genuine phenomena and those that are easily explainable. This approach not only empowers homeowners to address their fears but also fosters a deeper understanding of the natural world around them.

One of the first steps in embracing skepticism involves honing observation skills. When unusual noises or occurrences happen, it is vital to document these events meticulously. Keeping a journal that records dates, times, and descriptions of phenomena can help identify patterns or triggers. This practice can reveal natural explanations behind seemingly supernatural events, such as plumbing issues or electrical malfunctions. By systematically investigating these occurrences, individuals can gain clarity and reduce anxiety regarding their living environment.

Understanding psychological factors is another crucial aspect of skepticism. Human perception is often influenced by emotions and beliefs, which can skew interpretations of events. For instance, feelings of fear or anxiety can amplify the perception of a noise, transforming a simple creak into an ominous sign of a haunting. By recognizing these psychological influences, individuals can recalibrate their responses to unexplained occurrences. Engaging in mindfulness techniques or cognitive behavioral strategies can help mitigate the impact of fear, enabling a more rational evaluation of the situation.

Conducting a personal investigation armed with skepticism also entails employing the right tools and techniques. Utilizing basic equipment, such as digital voice recorders or infrared thermometers, can aid in capturing evidence that can be analyzed later. However, it is crucial to approach these investigations with a critical mindset. Electronic voice phenomena, for instance, might be misinterpreted sounds that are not paranormal in nature. Learning to use these tools effectively while maintaining a skeptical approach can lead to more accurate conclusions about what is truly happening in one's home.

Ultimately, embracing skepticism is about empowering oneself to confront the unknown with a rational mindset. By fostering a culture of inquiry, homeowners can explore their fears without succumbing to superstition. This approach not only aids in ruling out the possibility of hauntings but also cultivates a broader understanding of the world. It encourages individuals to seek answers rooted in reality, thus transforming a potentially frightening experience into an opportunity for personal growth and knowledge.